Dear

Adventurous
Heart

brandi marie

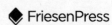 FriesenPress

One Printers Way
Altona, MB R0G 0B0
Canada

www.friesenpress.com

ISBN
978-1-03-914031-8 (Hardcover)
978-1-03-914030-1 (Paperback)
978-1-03-914032-5 (eBook)

1. POETRY, SUBJECTS & THEMES, LOVE & EROTICA

Distributed to the trade by The Ingram Book Company

Acknowledgements

I thank every heart who has held mine. Whether as a lover, or as a friend, you have all played a hand in inspiring my creativity to produce this collection of art, which exists in your hands now. So thank you, from the bottom of my heart.

I also thank each person who has shown up for me when my heart isn't in the best shape. You each provided me with love when I felt like my world had been stripped of it. Your kindness runs deep within me.

Lastly, I thank my own heart. My heart incessantly pulls me toward what always seems to scare me most, and what always seems to help me grow. I hope you all find a piece of your own hearts within these pages. I hope you can listen, as it is your own heart that speaks to you as you read my words.

iii

brandi marie

Instagram: @brandimariepoetry
Email: brandimariepoetry@gmail.com

I am not writing this one for anyone; everyone has their own heart to guide them. I am writing this one for me and my heart, yet with the hope that it helps someone else to decide to follow their own heart, wherever it may guide them.

Dear Adventurous Heart

Brandi Marie

Illustrations by
Rebecca Sawatzky &
Brandi Marie

Liam,

Thank you for supporting my dream and for opening up your heart and story with me over QOTD's. I hope you find relevance in these pages.

-B

Dear Adventurous Heart,

You have led me down some wondrous paths in our years together, and you undeniably have a mind of your own. Sometimes our desires are polar opposite, but when we do want the same thing, it's as if the entire world aligns—every star, every mountain, every ocean. You beat, and I exist. You feel, and I respond. You persist, and I grow. Your interests guide us to learn and to love new hearts, others' hearts. And sometimes we must hurt those hearts to outgrow and move forward; I understand that now. I also understand that going against you only makes every heart involved hurt more. I've learned to trust in you and to trust that your best interests align with mine. When I follow in the direction you point, I am never disappointed; although, I am always scared. But if we do not push through our fears, we will never blossom to a greater potential. You taught me that. So here is our journey, thus far, in times when we love, ache, and heal. In times when we fight, and in times when we thrive. I would like to thank you for all you have put us through, for I know I wouldn't be who I am today without your incessant desires guiding me through all sorts of adventures that are far from over.

Sincerely,
the girl who follows you
wherever you go

brandi marie

This is mostly about me,
But you may find,
I often write about you.

Table of Contents

DESIRE

noun
a longing or craving, as for something that brings satisfac-
tion or enjoyment:
a desire for love.

A desire for love exists
before we even learn what love is.
But once we taste love,
it becomes addicting.
We become addicted.
Like a drug,
the desire amplifies to a craving.
Sometimes we want love.
Sometimes we want love back.
It's usually only after we give it up
that we realize just how much
we crave love.

I create false realities in my head.

Like, what it would be like to be in a relationship with ___.

I feel him hold me as I'm falling asleep.

I hear his voice from my passenger seat.

All the while, waiting.

For him to notice me.

Or to realize I'm all he'll ever want or need.

But then I wake up to find out he's into ____.

Instead of me.

Me.

And I'm hurt.

Hurt that he didn't enjoy all that made-up time we spent together

Like I did.

Hurt that he was thinking of her in all the ways I was imagining him.

Then I blame him.

As if I spilled out all my feelings to him,

That he's unaware I have,

And he rejected me.

Me.

When I should be blaming myself.

For pretending.

For leading myself on.

For keeping quiet about my heart.

But when I do this, it makes me happy.

So he sees me as happy.

Without him.

He doesn't know that the very thought of him

Is what is making me happy.

It's all flowers and sex
And you in my head.
It's all beers and sunsets
And me in your bed.

But it isn't the action of him placing his right hand on her
left thigh as they drive down the highway, that I want.
For anyone could do that.
It's the feeling she gets when he does.

I'm looking for a hand
to fit in my back pocket.
I'm looking for a heart-shaped picture
in a locket.
I'm looking for an I-love-you note
in my wallet.
I'm not looking for you.

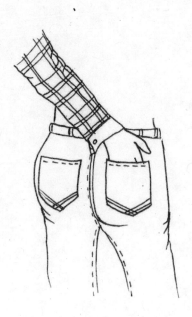

Waiting for someone to understand you is like fishing

    you have to be patient
    you have to keep waiting

Waiting for the right moment where peace and vulner-
ability collide

    you have to put yourself out there
    be confident and comfortable

As you are the worm on the hook hoping

    you have what it takes to hook another
    simply as who you are

    be patient
    keep waiting

The right fish will bite
you will be satisfied

I'm choosing to believe in you:
your existence
your perfection
Now, I suppose I don't have to:
your disappointment
my satisfaction
Yet, each time I try not to:
my disappointment
my decision
I continue to hold onto you:
your existence

my imagination

my
mouth
waters
at
the
very
thought
of
tasting
yours

I know he's not serious

And he's not entirely in my best interest

But I can't help being curious

When he's so good at remaining mysterious

I used to run from the boys
who would chase me during recess—
until one day
I walked up to you and said yes.
We used to run circles
around the ways which we felt
until one day you stopped me
and the next day I left.

I used to run from the boys
who would chase me during recess—
until one day you caught up,
and the next day I fell.
I broke your heart—
that you won't ever forget.
But you broke mine back;
now I live with regrets.

I used to run from the boys
who would chase me on the playground—
today, I still do;
I'm quite tough to tie down.

brandi marie

I like you better on the internet
I like to talk more when we text
And every time we've ever met
All you are is a disappointment

sometimes I can't tell
whether you're simply
passing pleasantries
or if your compliments
and kind remarks are
means to flirt with me

I'll be okay with either
conclusion but I'm
beginning to lean toward
the illusion that you're
into me because I'm so
into you like when you
get too close and I forget
what to do

my breathing is irregular
my heartbeat is the same
not to mention my mind
you've bent out of shape

I don't even know you
but God damn it I want to

if this is what it's like to not
know you at all, I can't wait
to feel what it's like when I
fall

I'd like to be held,
But I don't want to hold you back.
I'd like to be soothed,
But I won't ever rub your back.
I want to fall in love,
But I need it to be the truth.
I want to be yours,
But
I
Don't
Want
You.

You've entered my thoughts.

Which is weird.

Because my thoughts often include lines like:

That would never work.

And explanations like:

He's so much better off with her.

And reassurances like:

I wouldn't like that about him.

And reminders like:

I already have a boyfriend.

But you've entered my thoughts.

And I don't know what to do about them.

I can't exactly turn them off.

good
integrity
or
bad
intentions

I can't fall for any of you.

Because I'm hoping
That he realizes
I'm holding out for him.

And I'm hoping
That he realizes
I'm all he wants and needs.

But, so far,
He doesn't seem to want me.

Which is probably the only reason
Why I still want him.

For if he were to change his mind,
And want me one last time,
I'd probably go ahead
And change mine.

there's not a whole lot
more we can do to hurt
each other. so we might
as well do everything we
never had the chance to
when we were together.

Some days I get impatient
And wonder if I should text you
But it's only been one day since
And I know you need to rest soon

I'm writing too many poems
But I know I'm on your mind too
And I really ought to stop
I know she needs your time too

Part of me wants to do something brave
Once it was you to act the fool
But maybe you'll turn me down right back
After all it's my turn to show my heart too soon

We haven't mentioned a word since
I'm wishing that I could go back and undo
Or turn it all to pretend
A dream where you said you love me too

I'll always want everything you have:

> your thoughts
>
> your heart
>
> your soul
>
> your time

I always thought you wanted my everything too.

But maybe, you only wanted a few things of mine.

You're everything
        and so much more
I'm just not ready
        to open this door
I'll always need you
        but you know that
You get me
        and always have my back
You're my best friend
        that will never change
This connection we share
        also won't ever fade
Just remember one thing
        that I'll love you forever
Even when you're not mine
        it's my fault we aren't together
You're everything
        I'm looking for
I just hope you're still waiting
        when I open this door

brandi marie

I had a dream where you wanted me
Yet when I woke up, only one pair of feet
Were tangled in sheets of the bed
And although two pillows, lay only one head
I hate having dreams that leave me feeling misled

I shouldn't want to,
But I want to touch you.
I shouldn't need this,
But I need this closeness.
Out of all the things I shouldn't do,
They all seem to be revolving themselves
Around you.
Are you magnetic?
Or are you just like the sun?
Where I'm all your planets,
And you are my one.

I hoped it was you
The knock at my door
I hoped it was you
Behind me in queue at the store
I hoped it was you
Running fingers through my hair
I hoped it was you
Who caught my eye when he caught my stare
I hoped it was you
Riding shotgun in my jeep
I hoped it was you
Forever choosing to be with me

But it wasn't you
You are never mine
And I'll still hope for it to be you
Every time

the   i d e a   of you

gives me   b u t t e r f l i e s

and I want to   k e e p   it that way

so just   c l o s e   your eyes

even if for a   l i t t l e   while

I fell asleep
To the thought of
You holding me

My hands ran
Through my own hair
Pretending
That it was you there

Shuffled over to the left side
Leaving space
For you to lay
Right beside me

I fell asleep
So peacefully
By just the thought
Of you with me

& if you get me,
you get all fifteen of me
because I'm willing to be
all your fantasies

—the genie in me

you remind me of someone.

someone I never had the chance to truly be with.

and I fear

that if I were to be with you,

it would only be to take back my chance

at getting to be with him.

the party dies down
'til the last two up
          are you and I
I start to feel dead sober
as we lock our
          four brown eyes
I don't know what to say
and judging by the silence
          you don't either
so instead of speaking
we just stare deeper
          and deeper

brandi marie

I'm waiting for someone to tell me no.
To give me the red light.
The bad idea.
The please don't.
Otherwise, I just might.

my hand wanted to close itself around the man's arm that accidentally fell too close.

    instinctively.
        reflexively.
            naturally.

he was as much a stranger to me as the desire to touch someone would be.

    starved.
        deprived.
            craved.

in reality, he might have been nobody. but in my head, he was you, so I could be near somebody.

    longing.
        reaching.
            itching.

it fed me a drop of a type of tasting, which I had no idea I was craving.

    attention.
        relation.
            connection.

as this stranger walks away, I chase him. the same way I do when it comes to you.

    wistfully.
        pathetically.
            hopelessly.

~a familiar stranger

I want intimacy
and romance
two pairs of feet
and to hold hands
a smooth kitchen floor
for a slow dance
you opening my door
and me giving us a chance

being drawn to you:

>   it's like being charged or energized
>   an electric current
>   buzzing me back to life
>
>   it's like standing on the edge of a cliff
>   an adrenaline rush
>   paralyzed in place afraid to fall off of it
>
>   it's like getting pushed into a lake
>   a total shock
>   a refreshing place
>   until I can't breathe and need to resurface
>
>   as exciting
>   and enticing as it is

being drawn to you:

>   it's too temporary to be secure
>   it's overwhelmingly too much
>   it's too sweet to be pure
>   it's too fleeting to be love

When I see you in person, it's not that bad.
I keep my distance to remind myself
that things are different now between us.
But when you start up good conversations with me,
it becomes all too easy
to let go of my composure
and fall into the imagery of
what we could be.

I hate it when you say my name
It pulls at e v e r y heart string
I've spent years untying them from one another
They had tangled themselves into the lettering of
your name
Then six letters spill easily from your soft lips
And suddenly e v e r y hold I have on myself slips
I was so close
It's a shame
I love it when you say my name

I'm not supposed to focus on the kiss. It was harmless. I'm okay with that, honestly. I can take things harmlessly. But I'm still going to think about it.

You said maybe we shouldn't go on a late-night stroll because we'd end up doing more than just strolling. You said we should talk first. And we've been speaking quite frequently lately, but we haven't "talked" in over a year. So I picked you up after we had both gone home, and we talked.

"What do you want to talk about?" Now and again, I think you show interest toward me, but I write it off as me overthinking or over-hoping.

You think about me quite frequently as of lately.

"Me too."

You aren't ready for serious.

"I don't want to rush, not with us."

Between us there is certainly something.

"I can't look at you and feel nothing."

There's no such thing as just friends.

"Maybe we should try, before we try again."

"This night can't end without a kiss. I'm too curious. It'll be harmless. I'm just worried we won't be able to stop," you say.

We kiss.

It's innocent. It's tentative. It's sure. It's fragile. It's strong. It's honest. It's passion. It's butterflies. It's memories. It's unknown, uncharted. It's us. Our kiss. Our what must be millionth, yet feels like first.

I'm willing to bet, you're thinking about it too.

I don't mind waiting for you.

So long as you don't mind me,

holding

my

breath.

You tell me it's sexy when I bite my lip like that.
But if you'd simply let me,
I'd be busy biting yours.
I bet you'd think that's even sexier,
Wouldn't you?

maybe
we were never meant to be
or maybe
there
is
a
world
where we would've worked out
perfectly

I'm ready for warm weather,
That way when I'm alone with my thoughts,
I won't be cold.

And I'm ready for you whenever,
That way after I've gotten used to being warm,
I'll have you to hold.

We've parted ways more than once in the past.
A part of me went with you as we passed.
I miss those parts
Every minute we're apart,
But I kept parts of you too.

I partly felt whole when you left.
Because your parts filled the holes that were left.
We used to part lips.
Now we are separate,
But you held the parts of me that you took.

I partly think this because you think of me.
For the most part I believe that you're starting to see
That the worst part has passed,
And the best part is not the past.
And I'm willing to take part in a future with you.

Now, I've done my part in telling you this.
So, please, play your part and tell me you admit
That we're dressed the part,
Apart from being undressed.
Our private parts are exposed, just like us.

I'm thinking you
And I'm thinking me
I'm thinking us
And I'm thinking we

I'm thinking could
And I'm thinking should
I'm thinking would
If you understood

That I think of us
All the damn time
And I think we must
Give one last try

I think this could
Be the right time
Because I know
I want you as mine

the wind rushes through blades of grass
    the way I imagine your hands in my hair

the waves kiss and kiss the sand
    and you don't kiss me at all—how is that fair?

Dear a Former Lover,

I know we've been apart for quite a while now. And we've each experienced our separate lives. I'm no longer (and haven't been for some time) someone you tell things to. Whether that be how your day was, or what troubles you late at night. As you aren't that person for me either. We've each found other people on our journeys. But I'd like to get to know you, again.

We could start small, if you're willing to hear about my day periodically, and exchange stories. I would like to re-establish a friendship with you. I do not, however, wish to do so under any false pretences.

I'll want more. More than just small talk. More than group-setting hangouts. And more than just a friendship.

I would like to get to know you first, for all that's changed. But people change as much as feelings do, so I would like to know if you believe that too.

> Sincerely,
> and hopefully,
> a Future Lover

Here I am,
thinking:
>   *she is better for you.*
But what if
you're thinking that:
>   *he's better for me.*
We could both be wrong,
Couldn't we?

I'm wasting my time on tasteless guys,

While I wait for your heart to decide to take mine.

It wouldn't have just been the idea of you that I fell for, if you had let me fall for the real thing. But I'm beginning to become glad that you didn't. Every time I get close to you, I lose a sense of sight, leading me to forget the reasons we shouldn't be together anymore. Now that I'm away from you, I can easily list all our differences and opposing desires in this life. And the underlying truth is just that: we don't want the same things in life other than each other. But as much as there is something that always pulls us back to one another, it also always tears us apart. Yet despite all logic, all realistic thoughts, and two broken hearts, I'll always still love you.

LOVE

noun

a profoundly tender, passionate affection for another person.

Love is, more often than not, impossible to define.
It is how I am yours, and you are mine.
Yet, it isn't possession.
And it isn't always larger over time.
Sometimes love blossoms from hate.
After crossing that very thin line.
Love is a bottle of Corona,
fizzing from finding its slice of lime.
Love is a gust of wind creating music,
allowing those ornaments to chime.
We mistake love for being a destination,
but love will always be the climb.

I consider myself to be one of the luckiest people
I have found and loved more than just the one
I have met more mates for my soul than what is defined as
a soulmate
I have lived and loved and laughed with them all
I may have lost more loves than my heart is capable
of losing
But I have also loved more hearts than my hands are
capable of holding
I have found and loved more than just the one
And I consider myself one of the luckiest people

Love is not a destination
Especially once you get there

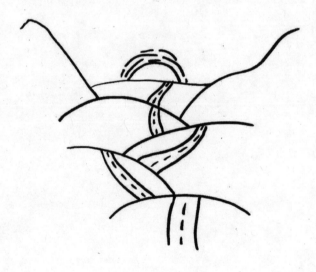

You fall out of love, and you think
There's no way I could find a connection like this again
There is no one else I could say these words to
And mean it like I do with him

And then you meet someone
And it starts slow
But you begin to notice this slight change of inflection in
your voice
And you realize they have a nickname
You speak two words to them
That mean nothing to anyone else
Yet it's code for I love you
You forget the words you spoke to the first one
That made you feel this way
But you don't forget the feeling

And that's how you know
It is possible to move on
Fall out of love with him
And it is possible
To fall in love again

Crisp autumn air
Sunlight
peeking through leaves
I fill my lungs
I feel the breeze
She's brushing her fingertips
through strands of my hair
More radiant
in this golden-hued
blue hour
I watch as burnt leaves
let go
of what they've been holding onto since
Spring
One in particular
lays down on the earth
Ready
to re-flower
The sun in her morning glory
climbs above the mountaintops
as I climb down to the water
She tickles the surface
who giggles in glitter
And with my eyes closed
I can still see
she has risen slow and graceful
her light
reveals what has always been beautiful
And the only thing I have to compare it to
is the way I feel
when I'm with you

I remember meeting you,
And all the stars, they split in two.
They showed me just what love could do.
All because I fell for you.

I wasn't scared travelling Australia with my best friend.

I wasn't scared moving to Jasper for six months by myself.

I wasn't even that scared once I got to Cambodia.

But moving out with you,

I'm terrified.

Because all those other adventures were temporary.

And this,

With you,

It could be permanent.

And I've never had so much to lose.

I'm trying to stretch and sip my coffee at the same time.
Like how I try not to reply too quick or too slow
Or stare at you as you walk by.
I'm trying to figure out what I should do for the rest of
my life.
I've gotten as far as hoping it's with you.
And if it is,
It doesn't matter what else in the world I get to call mine.

It's as if we were the type of garden
one buys flowers for and simply
re-plants them in front of their home.

    ; beautiful

    ; breath-taking

    ; impossible to upkeep.

When our last petal fell, I sat on my
knees in front of that garden, willing
it to turn back into the beauty it once
was. I tried to learn how to plant
new, different gardens, but none as
enchanting as ours. Then after all
that time, you came around, bringing

    ; the sun

    ; the soil

    ; the seeds

    ; yourself.

And our garden grew back even more
beautiful, and stronger than the first time.

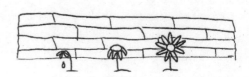

I could stare up at the blue sky for quite some time,
Yet it's never as enrapturing as the abyss of your blue eyes.
I could lose track of the time relaxing in the soft sand,
Yet time seems to stop when I'm held in your hands.
I could drink a glass of water, any hour of the day,
Yet my thirst for your lips seems to never go away.
I could jump into a lake under the hot summer sun,
Yet there isn't a time of year I wouldn't jump into
your love.

My body, to me, is just like a home.
Yet, not stuck in one place,
It takes me where I like to go.
I'm never too lost, and I'm never alone.
As long as I've got me,
I'm safe, and I'm home.

Then, one day, as I'm walking,
You come along.
I suddenly know a new place I belong.
You change my views,
You crawl inside my bones.
We both find a heart, a soul,
And a home.

I'm not really great at playing the guitar,
but my fingers too easily
pluck the strings
tying my heart to yours.

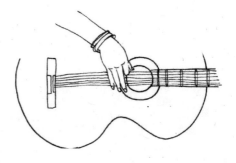

Don't kiss her too soon.
Make her wait.
Make yourself wait.
Drag out the suspense.
Drag out the mystery.
Drag out the intention.
And don't kiss her if there isn't one.

Kiss a girl who feeds you good intentions.
And when you do kiss her,
For the first time:
Keep it simple.
Kiss her softly.
Just once.
Leave your presence lingering on her lips.
Leave her wanting more.
And then don't leave her.

Love her.
And keep loving her.
And keep kissing her.

uncontrollable

vast

untamed

wide

unpredictable

fast

unknown

wild

Each one of these things lives in the sky,
and each one of these things comes to life in your eyes.
The blue holds the unknown, and is ferociously vast.
While the clouds roll on in and seem impossibly fast.
You're so unpredictable, you cannot be controlled.
Even the weather-man's forecast is wildly unknown.
But each time you roll in as the clouds in my sky,
my heart beats untamed as my arms open wide.
Love is defined by each one of these things,
and each one of these things is defined by our love.
So just as the sky and the weather above,
I cannot control how I feel for your love.

I remember
a few nights after I met you
I was in my room
doing yoga
and then reading poetry
completely clueless
as to how much
you would soon mean to me

snow in September

I'm expectant of my shock
And surprised by my delight
I have yet to see the colours of autumn
Before experiencing these streets coated in white
Something meant to happen gradually
Suddenly happens all at once
It's just like meeting you
As I try quickly to adjust
It's a little bit like magic
And quite a bit like chance
But if it's going to snow in September
I may just have to ask you to dance
So won't you take me by the hand
Drag me headfirst into this summer storm
And if you promise to keep me safe
I'll promise to keep you warm

brandi marie

I want to love you.
I want to buy you sweaters.
I want to leave parties with you.
I want to cook dinner for you.
I want to hold you.
I want to sing all my songs for you.
I want to read books with you.
I want to have dinner at your mom's.

I want you to love me.
I want you to be brave.
I want you to face the world with me.
I want to show you it's okay to be afraid.
I want you to touch me.
I want you to follow your heart.
I want you to be proud of me.
I never want us to be apart.

we're taking off like
an airplane in the middle of the night
in a vast dark sky
over all those city lights

from down below
they'll see our shooting star
'cause they don't know what we are
they've never felt like this before

they've never felt like us before

Love is in the moon
Love is in the sun
Love is found inside
Each and everyone

Love is in his eyes
Love is in her heart
Love will stay beside you
Even when love falls apart

Love may become lost
But love can always be found
In everything we do
And everyone who sticks around

Well, you have officially and successfully checked off
my checklist.

Aced it.
Passed with flying colours.
Congratulations.

You would have passed sooner, if I had written my
checklist sooner.

Procrastination.
Fear.
My apologies.

Potentially, I hadn't written it previously
Due to disappointment when others:

Failed.
Flunked.
Broke my heart.

And because I had to go through my own lows before you:

Taught me to fly.
To believe.
To love.

But I have it written down now, as:
"What I'm looking for,"
Except, when I wrote it, I had one thing in mind:

End game.
Forever.
You.

close your eyes
and picture a sky
now paint it in colour
then explain to me why

take my hand
before jumping in the deep end
share with me your rush
so I may begin to understand

tell me your secrets
that no one else knows
take me to places
no one but you goes

map out your dreams with me
and I'll map mine right back
colour in a world with me
we don't have to live in white and black

I watched you fall in love today
Your eyes spoke words you wouldn't say
Forever is a long ways away
But I watched you fall in love today

I watched you fall in love today
Your hand in mine so easily
You won't admit but I can see
I watched you fall in love today

I watched you fall in love today
You asked me if it was okay
I laughed and said I think you're great
I watched us fall in love today

I watched us fall in love today
The colours all came out to play
The world is such a beautiful place
Because we both fell in love today

You say I'm out of your league
I'm too pretty

But I'm just me

You say I could do better than you
Maybe I don't want to

Maybe I want you

I say you're too good to me
Too kind, too giving

But don't you see

That you and I fit perfectly
It's just easy

Being you and me

we sat really close on this bench
and I wasn't really sure what that meant
back then
but I get it now
and I really wish we could go back somehow

Lately, I haven't been into testing the waters before I dive.

And you've been there to join me, side by side.

Taking on temperatures together, below what we are used to.

Jumping in head-first, to an unexplored blue.

art is about creating what ceased to exist before the artist
brought it to life.

just like love.

when two people decide to be together,

they create art.

they create love.

passion is to love, what paper is to art;

nothing.

blank.

empty.

non-existent.

until you decide to create something out of it,

until you decide to love.

love

like art,

does not exist on its own;

it is created.

every

single

ounce

of

me

wants to run away

which is how

I

know

this is probably real

and

I

ought

to

stay

I believe that we evolve into who we are
every time we allow a new soul to enter our hearts.
We are given pieces of other people's existence,
and that affects how we perceive, how we listen.
It alters the beating patterns of our hearts,
I am who I am because you are who you are.

Sometimes I find myself wishing that I could hear what people are saying about us.

What an odd wish to have, I think.

Because don't I already know?

Isn't that why it took me so long to love you in the first place?

I over-care what outside people think.

And the worst part,

Is that I think I know what those people are thinking.

What is she doing?

She's way too good for him.

She could have any guy she wants.

How did he deceive her?

The answer to all these questions,

Is that I stopped listening.

I stopped caring about all the words I never truly heard.

And I began to listen within.

Now the worst part is that it took me so long.

And the best part?

The best part is how I no longer believe those doubts existed inside anyone's mind but my own.

The best part is how they no longer exist,

And we do.

I believe in love at first sight
I also believe that that isn't always how it goes
Some loves are gradual
Like the receding of rock
From a constant movement of water
Revealing its grandest waterfall
Love can strike you all at once
Like jumping off a cliff
To be entirely engulfed
By the frigid water waiting below
Or love can sneak up on you
Like a season
Like a slow wade into the ocean
Neither is right nor wrong
But I feel grateful to say that
I have had the chance
To experience both
Possibly there is someone out there
Who holds a love as evidence
That I could be wrong
But in my experience
One type of love is fast and bright
Like lightning
And over all too soon
While the other is patient and promising
Longer lasting
And true

If you can't thrash around in the water,
Clinging to a buoy like it's your last hope,
And still call it swimming,

Then you can't call whatever it is you're doing with him
Love.

Every love that wilted
Or walked out on me
Left inside
A hole
No peace
But then you came
And burrowed in
You filled that space
I don't know when
Some point in time
I said okay
Then you were mine
Here to stay
The hole is still there
But now it glows
From a light only you
And love expose

I developed some mad independence.
And I did that all on my own.
It was my goal.
Then I met you.
You are independent too.
But I often find myself
Not wanting to do the things I love
Alone anymore.
I'd much rather share them with you.

I've put it on a scale
And inside a measuring cup
I've stuck it in the sand
To watch it fall or stand up

I've brought it to the gym
To see how much it weighed
I've run it down the street
To see how fast it raced

I've dropped it in the ocean
To watch it sink or float
I've set it on fire
Will it explode or smoke?

The one thing which I've learned
Is there's no way to measure
A love like yours and mine
Is a weightless type of treasure

brandi marie

You imagine it
Your whole life
What it will feel like
When he's in it
You imagine roses
And chocolate maybe
A hand to hold
Talk about having a baby
Rings
And proposals
What you'll say to each other in vows
Feeling steady and hopeful
But when you grow up
And spend far too many nights alone
You end up realizing
That love isn't at all what you imagined
Or hoped
Sure, you get a rose
After you screamed at one another
Over something stupid
Like who steals the covers
And you call way too late
To get together
For a midnight ice-cream date
The rings are too expensive
And the baby is too intimidating
To even think about
Aren't we too young to move out of the basement
As for the vows
Those are special no matter what you call them
It's when one of you is half asleep

And the other wakes you up
Just to say
I love the way you help my parents with housework
And then someone farts
And you aren't embarrassed
You just laugh
Like it was the funniest thing in the universe
Love isn't perfect
So if you're still trying to imagine what it will feel like
Picture yourself being the most goofy, authentic version
of you that you have
And then picture someone sharing that moment with you
And being completely themselves too

Stop that
You know what I'm talking about
All that
I'm forever alone
No one will ever love me
I'm not _____ enough
Bullshit
And admit that you need to learn to love yourself
Because if you don't
No one is going to do it for you

We had resistance
You weren't my type
And I was too good for you

We had tension
We knew better
But we wanted to get to know each other anyways

We had release
We realized
It was never going to work out

Then we had love
We gave in to the passion
And ignored what anyone else thought of us

It won't all come naturally
You're going to have to teach him that
When you cry
You don't want him to continuously ask you why
You just need him to sit beside you
And bring you a Kleenex box

You're going to have to teach him that
Just because you asked him to bring you ice cream
Doesn't necessarily mean you want the same flavour you
had last time

You're going to have to teach him that
If he wants you to sleep over
You're going to need more than a moment's notice
Hello
Girl needs to pack a toothbrush
And probably eighteen other essential items

You're going to have to teach him that
Just because none of his past girlfriends critiqued
his kissing
Doesn't mean there isn't any room for improvement

But between all the teaching
Don't forget to learn
There is nothing worse
Than a take-without-giving relationship

Take your time
Don't be afraid to be alone
Figure out who you are
Before you go looking for someone to define you

Everyone wants to be in it
And everyone loves to feel loved
People are so quick to comment
But few enjoy being judged

They say the truth hurts
And that love makes us blind
But when your best friend tells you he's wrong
All you can feel is undermined

Is it desperation
That leads us astray
Or immanent loneliness
That makes us afraid?

You know when you know
When two people aren't right
But when you are one half
It's like a loose-flying kite

You lose all control
As you flail in the wind
But the fall saves your knees
It's your heart that gets skinned

If only you listened
When they told you the outcome
But we can only learn from ourselves
Especially when it comes to love

Love is slow burning like a single-wick candle in
the evening
Like a single malt scotch poured over one single ice cube
Like a hot bubble bath on a night in December
Like a long kiss in the car when the rain blurs
the windshield

Love is slow rising like lingering fog lifting off the ground
Like the climb of a roller coaster before the big drop
Like the build of anticipation as you clamber up
a mountain
Like watching the sun over ocean waves coming up

Love is fast paced like a wild cat gaining on its
getaway prey
Like jumping off a dock to be engulfed by frigid water
Like an airplane taking off and the pop in your eardrums
Like that same roller coaster racing with the force
of gravity

Love is fast tracked like moving in together for the
first time
Like shopping the day before Christmas
Like quarantining with your lover for more than
two weeks
Like falling asleep mid-movie and waking up to
the ending

We never quite know how much
pressure is being applied to the gas
Because love can burn slow, and
love can race fast

brandi marie

I have learned how to love doing everything myself
How to adhere to my desires
And follow my heart

I have learned to spend time on things I'm passion-
ate about
How to relish in my writing
And believe in my art

But now that I have you, there are new things I have
to learn
How to share my time with someone
And still make time for me

I have learned that loving you has brought new light into
my heart
How simply being next to you can
Bring out the best parts of me

It's when he touches your hand
And you feel it in your stomach
It's when he first says your name
And you start to hear trumpets

It's when you listen to an old song
But he's given it new meaning
It's when he silently kisses you
But inside you're screaming

It's when he first asks you out
And you've over-practiced how to say yes
And then you're both at a loss
At what happens next

It can be so enchanting
And not just when you're young
What truly makes it magic
Is when you fall deep in love

Let's get back to the place where
Fairy tales and true love exist
Even if we're playing pretend
Even if for just a little bit

When was the last time someone asked you to count the
cars of a train
Or to look up at the sky and see the pictures the
clouds paint?
When did you last curl up next to someone and make up
names for the constellations of stars
Or feel the tender kisses that make art out of your scars?
When was the last time someone challenged
your imagination
Or told you just because you're moving out doesn't mean
you have to grow up?
It's important to have someone who makes you feel young
And touches your heart so well that you relearn to believe
in love.

Love is a cycle
You'll go through it all
You'll want him so bad
You won't care how you fall

You'll love him and love him
But it won't be enough
And maybe one day
You will fall out of love

You'll cry and you'll scream
You'll pretend you're okay
You'll do something stupid
And regret it one day

But then you will breathe
And you'll do things for you
You'll realize what you don't need
After all you went through

You'll be so content
You may not realize
Just what it means
When you fall for new eyes

You might try to hold back
But let me assure you
Love is a cycle
Worth going through

FIGHT

noun

a battle or combat

any contest or struggle.

Sometimes we fight for love
And sometimes we fight while we're in love
Sometimes the fight is worth it
And sometimes it's best to give up

There's something that I should say
And nothing that I can do
You can choose to walk away
Yet every time I'll still choose you

Now I know I'm out of line
But I hope you'll want me too
See I can't seem to change my mind
When all it thinks about is you

My heart beats faster when you're near
And makes me act like quite the fool
Then slows right down when you're not there
Because it craves to beat for you

We may have broken in the past
And both tried on someone new
But I believe what's old can last
And still believe in me and you

I'm a very loving person
to someone willing
to take it all.

But, I'm not so forgiving
to someone who only wants
to take it all off.

Take my heart
and I will fall,
hard.

Take my clothes,
and the first door will
close.

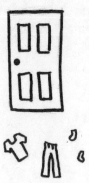

I left you
so that I didn't
need you.
I left you
for independence.
And I found it.

Then I lost you.

And I found him.

Now I've lost the ability
to be dependant.
And I'm terrified
to love someone
I
don't
need.

And here I am, googling the lyrics to a song titled, "I Don't Miss You," trying to convince myself of this. But really just relating to the lie. Yet I'm still hoping it prevents me from texting you.

Why are you here again anyways?

Don't you know that your name lighting up my phone screen takes me right back to the beginning?

And I was doing so well. I was rid of you. Or I thought I was, until you showed up again. Could you either stop, and never speak to me, or stick around? Like actually?

Because if you wanted me and wanted to stay, I could use you right now. I could be ready, finally. Now. For you. And that's saying a lot, because I don't think I could say that about anyone else.

So figure out what you want because I already know what I want. And if we don't want the same thing, then figure out how to let me go. Because I can't keep doing this. It hurts too much.

I have a lot of love built up inside me
And no one to give it to
It's been accumulating since the day I left you
And I don't believe it's at all a matter
Of not knowing what to do
But that I'd rather not give it up
Unless I'm giving it back to you

Letting go
Of control
Isn't something
I know
All I know
Is control's
Something
I can't let go

Moving on
From your love
Isn't something
I wish
All I wish
Is for a piece
Of your love
To move on with

I walk home from your place past dark
and take your coat to keep me from the
cold air and my thoughts on how I wish
she would leave because you're holding
her   instead   of   me

I'm searching to find balance.
That's all life is about, after all,
Isn't it?

A balance of season
        of sunshine and rain
A balance of time
        of asleep and awake
A balance of emotion
        of pure joy and raw pain

I'm searching to find balance,
But I've already found it in all these things.

So how do I find balance between
        withholding for someone special
        and holding someone to feel special?

One of the worst questions you may ever have to ask
someone is,
"Are we okay?"
Because if you're the one asking,
Chances are, you don't have much say.
Not to mention, you likely already know the answer.
And hopefully, it has nothing to do with her.

Where is the line between,

"It's not too late,"

And, "the moment has passed"?

Because there is so much I have yet to say,

But time seems to move all too fast.

If I break yours
It doesn't make mine whole
If I break yours
I break mine
It's inevitable

My arms are crossed,
Across my stomach.
My stomach's in knots,
Not that you'd notice.
"But know this," I say,
Say to your green eyes,
"I'm not here to play around,
Or round out any lies.
So lie next to me,
In my arms, in my bed.
I bet that's what we need,
Needless the doubts in our heads."

okay, but
what if we pretended like
we've
never
met,
and just . . .
tried again?

react you may
react you will
your jealousy gives me such a chill

a chill which burns just like a flame
I did nothing wrong
yet still feel shame

across the couch
I stare at you
but without recognition so I ask who

who could act the way you did
you fought my battles
as if I were the kid

your temper tantrum tells the tale
this may sound sexist
but you're quite the male

I will love you back together,
because I can see you've fallen apart.
Then I will love you 'til forever,
even after you've broken my heart.

what if you don't like me
after we have sex
and when I open up
I'm an emotional wreck
what if I say something wrong
that turns us into a mess
what if I break your heart
what then
what happens next?

what if you lay down and I keep you up
because I can't sleep
and when I lay on your chest
I can't seem to breathe
what if we put our hearts together
and they don't align after they meet
what if we fall apart
would we simply never speak?

but what if we fall in love
the two of us are meant to be
and what if we spend a lifetime
simply as just you and me?

the sunflower holds its popularity
regardless of how often she wilts
and re-blooms yet we still fear that
we   will   fade

I always want what I don't have
I overthink and under plan
I say one thing then change my mind
I test your heart and waste your time
Yet you stay put and comfort me
I don't know why I crave to bleed
I wish my heart could feel at peace
Instead I push until you leave

I have always been afraid to feel
held back or tied down by someone
but I guess I was too busy
feeling like I found someone
I could let go of my fears with
I didn't realize you were experiencing
all the same fears
and I was the one
holding you back and tying you down

I apologize for growing unfair
I ought to believe in you
And in the fact that you care
I just get so in my head sometimes
To a space without you there
It all seems so real to me
Until I realize you're left unaware

I know what I said,
        but you know what you did.
        You changed the game.
And now you don't want things to change?

How can you ask me to throw away that amount of
        self-respect?
        Did you think I would do it?
What did you expect?

That you could introduce me to this other girl?
        That we'd both be happy
        living in your world?
Because that's not how the world works.

But you knew that already,
        didn't you?
        Why else
would you try to hide it for so long?

I just don't understand
        how you can feel you've done nothing wrong
        when I feel like a dirty, disgusting fool
too trusting for her own good.

How can you be okay with that?

As long as you get what you want,
        and I get nice and wet,
        who needs pride
when there's no dignity to protect?

As per
The girl
You think
Is going to
Change
The way
You play
Your game:

I hope she hurts you.
I hope she breaks your heart.
I hope you have one.
I hope you fall apart.

I've gone ahead in deciding to hate you. At least for a little while. And I know you were first to call dibs on creating distance, but then I thought, why let you have all the fun? You're clearly already having your fun, you know, with her. And I wonder if her boyfriend thinks of you in the same way that I do. Because I don't know about him, but I find your true colours to be quite repulsive. Although, I suppose he doesn't have the best sense of judgment if he's with a girl who would sleep with you. Kudos to her; God only knows that I couldn't do it. I'm well aware of how petty my words may come across, but I believe my bitterness is justified by your lack of owning up to your actions. And I may be full of temporary hatred, but are you really worthy of permanence, after all?

I think we both tried to be
What the other needed

But in the end

We could give each other
What we needed best

By leaving

"Could you give him a message for me?"
She asked after the flare of concern crossed her eyes.
"Tell him, he'd better treat my girl right."
But as she finished, she sighed.

Message and all, he couldn't treat me right if he tried.
It's a bit of a shame, and I'm ashamed that I cried.

It's hard not to be petty.
And it's hard not to hate you.
But something in you just tells me,
there's no way I can trust you.
Your fake love offends me;
I'm not trying to be rude.
I won't just let you lie to me,
through lips that bleed no truth.
So call me crazy if you'd like;
Tell your friends to hate me too.
And call me late when you get lonely;
I won't pick up.
Not if it's you.

I would love it if you were the one to make me shine brighter than the sun. It could be just you and I against all odds in space and time. But sometimes, I think a little too hard of the truth to the desires of my heart. I need to run both far and free, with room to grow, exponentially. I cannot have hands containing my fire. I need oxygen to feed my flames higher. I love the idea that you are the one to not only help me grow but also to teach me to love. I just can't help but wonder if you're holding me back. If without you, I'd be better off. Deep down I think I know that. So for now we will dance, we will laugh, we will sing. But keep in mind that one day I will spread out my wings. I don't mean to hurt you, to cause grief or heartache. And I hope one day you'll understand why I am this way. I hope, come that day, I too, will understand, why I feel so held back in the arms of a man.

Goodbyes are easier

When you grow less attached

So I push you away slowly

Before I never look back

I don't believe you understand
what goes on between me and boys
I don't like to touch their bodies
until I've touched their hearts
I like to keep all my clothes on me
until they learn my innermost naked parts
two people can each be special
yet still cease to fall like stars
my last he-loves-me-not rose petal
falls from my hand as we fall apart
I don't believe you understand
what goes on between me and boys
I give each one a fair chance
whilst blocking out the noise
they say we'll never last
and I refuse to hear that voice
so I play at your romance
for some time it fills my void
then I decide it's our last dance
they were right of my wrong choice
maybe you do understand
what goes on between me and boys

brandi marie

I'd like to introduce myself
I'm still getting over someone else
It's not that I'm not interested
I'm just busy comparing you to him

When you start a fire for someone other than yourself,
and when they choose not to stick around to help, one of
two things happen next.

First, your fire flickers out without a witness,
without love.
And you are left uncovering yourself from the ashes of
hopelessness in the dark.
Nothing left, not even a spark.

Or your fire is left unattended,
uncared for.
And in the heat of that loneliness, your flames catch hold
of everything in its raging grasp.
You light up a whole forest in your dangerous path.

When you start a fire for someone other than yourself,
it is only going to damage you, unless they stick around
to help.

brandi marie

There's this tension between us
It never seems to give
I ask if you feel this
Before letting you in
But the idea of us
It's too much for you to take
So you leave
And I hope you know it's a mistake

You had an apartment with her. Not actually, but hear me out. Your relationship was a home before you broke up. Then that home felt empty when you were in it alone. So you invite me over because we've also built a home in the past and you thought I could bring that feeling back. But that didn't work.

So you called her. And she returned. But while you were busy asking her to come back home, you forgot to ask me to leave.

You shut me in a closet while you let your life with her go on. As if I didn't exist. As if I meant nothing to you. As if you never wanted me in the first place.

And I'm just so sorry.

Sorry to be such an inconvenience to you both. I should've stayed in that closet so she wouldn't have had to watch me leave her home. I should've snuck out when no one was around and pretended like nothing had ever happened in her absence. I shouldn't have had feelings about the situation. But like you wanted her to come back, I prayed that you would want me.

I shouldn't have ever loved you. But I do.

He had too many skeletons
in his closet.

And that wouldn't have been an issue,

If I didn't walk right into them
when I opened the front door.

He Liked the Yellow Dress

I'll admit
I made a mess
Of you and I;
I should've worn the yellow dress.

I'll admit
That I impressed
The wrong guys;
I should've worn the yellow dress.

I'll admit
I thought less
Of what you thought;
I should've worn the yellow dress.

I'll admit
That I regret
A lot since then;
I should've worn the yellow dress.

I'll admit
The green was nice,
But I still wish
I'd worn the yellow dress.

dormant dead butterflies
rage in their shadows for you
stirring in their graves
hearing the familiar sound
of your voice
ghosts of feelings flutter
haunted memories swarm
inside my stomach
confused whether to remain
extinct
or to rejoice

Like You

It's guys like you that make him so desirable.

When he's everything you're not,
and you can't measure up to him in the slightest.
When you're getting to know me,
with all the wrong questions.
And I'm picturing him,
with all our better conversations.
When you have more to say,
yet he still has more to offer.
When we have more in common,
but
he's
got
me.

He's got me.

And I don't know how he did it,
but it was nothing
like you.

I stole something from you that could only go unnoticed
if I replaced it for you.
But I kept what was mine, and held onto yours too.
That wasn't ever the intention, it's just the
unwanted truth.
I crept in at night to replace what I stole.
But you lay awake, and you knew what I know.
I broke your heart by not giving mine up.
I gave yours back, but that wasn't enough.
The hole I created in you was the mess.
And the way that I left you is the part I regret.
I should've put something in place to replace what I stole.
A heart for a heart, not a hole for a hole.

Blame should not be spread, only taken in retrospect.

As I move all my shit out of our old basement suite
I realize just how little you contributed
To this so-called, two-way street

What was I to you? A place to lay your shoes when you quit wearing them? A roof over your head when the rain refused to relent? Was I the cat you leave at home when you want to go out all weekend? Was I the girl you thought would forgive you, again and again? You thought that things would end a little bit differently, didn't you? Or perhaps you thought that things would never end. Well, the joke's on you. 'Cause I grabbed my shoes. I left our roof to burn, and I took the cat too. There is no one left to forgive you.

I am the girl who everyone wanted you to be with,
      to settle down with.
Everyone, that is,
      except you.

you would've loved this
it's adorable
it's cozy
so far off from the city
you would've loved this
sipping coffee on the balcony
not worrying about reality
you would've loved this
walking through the autumn colours
falling deeper for each other
you would've loved this
homemade chili and a glass of wine
drunken giggles losing track of time

but you can't love this
can't you see
that you would've loved this
but you should've loved me

The breeze always seems to be heard before it is felt
Like the opposite of the natural warning signs of the
human condition
When something is about to go wrong
You always feel it first
There is no silence in the birds' chirp
There is no rustle in the trees' leafy branches
Like soft maracas going off in the distance
There is no siren of what is about to be felt
There is only you
And the uncomfortability that something very bad is
about to happen

I told you all that I didn't want,
right from the start.
Yet, you didn't think to walk away
when I described, in detail,
all that you are.

you left her
and slept with me
that was supposed to fucking mean something

when we woke up
you went back to her
and you expect me to be something other than hurt

you apologized
with unsympathetic eyes
am I supposed to buy into such lies?

you are not sorry
and neither is she
forgive me for thinking you gave a damn about me

Same old story. Brand new time. He said he'd change. He
fed you lies.
Every girl wants a bad guy who's good only for her.
Someone who lays down his walls and takes off
his armour.
But regardless of what he's wearing, people never
truly change.
He could step into a whole new light, yet underneath still
be the same.
So if he sleeps around, but he "stopped" for you,
Don't buy that shit; don't be a fool.
I'll bet he makes you dinner, brings you flowers.
Invites you to his place only to keep you up for hours.
He's selling something. He's telling lies.
But you're the girl, you're not supposed to buy.
So take your pride and tell him no.
Pack your bags and then go home.
They always want to change, but they never truly can.
And you're too busy trying to convince a boy
That he ought to be a man.

I'm
still
holding
onto
him
much
tighter
than
I'd
like
to
admit.

your name is carved

into my skin.

and if I could figure out where,

I might stand a chance

at scratching

it out.

I cannot be who you should be
or who you should be with
when people are watching
if you won't be that person
when they stop

alcohol takes the cake
she made me say things I didn't mean to say
okay
I meant them
but I didn't mean for them to come out that way
I meant to wait
I meant to have patience
I meant not to say
That inside I'm here waiting for you
because that's not fair to you
because that's not fair to her either

I'm not a perfectly good girl,
But I don't want to be the bad guy.
I'm more accustomed to goodbyes,
But I don't want to feed you bad lines.

Like:
It's not you, it's me.
It's just bad timing.
It's not you, I swear.
I truly do care.

Bad guy,
Good lie.

I'm just so pissed off that you did this.

You didn't even leave any room for forgiveness.

You took from me, my best friend in the process.

And that's hardly what the hardest part is.

You lied so much I'm surprised you can stand.

You lied that you and I stood any kind of a chance.

You lied when you said I was the only one.

Even if you wished that were true, it wasn't.

Now I can't help but wonder if it was all just a lie.

You pretended to be the one, but deep down you are not
that guy.

You say all these words and you ask for my forgiveness.

But your actions are what hurts.

The truth is you don't want shit, isn't it?

You make small talk with me as if nothing happened.

As if we can be friends, and I just cannot fathom

the idea of allowing you entry into my heart.

If you recall the last time I let you hold it, you tore

it apart.

Whatever you do, don't forget what you did.

You made your bed.

Now go do what you do best,

And lie in it.

sometimes we put so much into fixing someone else
that it isn't until they leave,
we realize we've only broken ourselves.

I'm in a dark room
alone
and I know this because
I can find all four walls
with my bare, panicked hands
I can find the marble floor
with my lifeless, defeated body
but I can't find you
you're not in this dark room
I'm alone

I don't even have a heart-shaped necklace to lay to rest in my jewelry box next to all my other exes.

—graveyard for heartbreak

cobwebs 2.0

there are cobwebs on my pillowcase
your arms wrap me up
but I lay awake
there are strings pulling up
the corners of your face
those same strings tie me up
but not in an embrace
there are cobwebs on my pillowcase
your eyelids flutter
as your lips form shapes
you mumble yet I make out
"what will it take?"
I stare at you through silence
who takes up too much space
despite my lack of response
you press into me and wait
all the while all I wish is to
clear the cobwebs from my pillowcase

You've never tried to fall in love.

I've never tried when I fall in love.

And now you're trying,
You're falling in love.

While I'm trying to fall in love.
Don't you see?

Trying something new,
vs.
Trying too hard with you.

Why do I blame you
for something he did?
Why do I like
having him in my head?

Listen to the rain
And tell me something
If I was your favourite person
Why cause me such pain?

Stand in the wind
Take one deep breath in
Let out the truth
Let it come from within

Lie in your bed
But don't lie to me
I hope sleeping alone
Helps you see more clearly

You are a liar
A cheater
A fake
Now you must lie in the bed
You so carelessly made

tell me your secrets
tell me your sins
what other girls
are you getting with
you could speak now
or keep it all in
but I will find out
and then who will win?

With every thrust of your body into hers
A new bruise formed on mine
Deep in my trust
My respect
My pride
Until you achieved satisfaction
And all I was left with
Were prominent welts and wounds
Throbbing like her thighs
Bleeding more abruptly than I could ever cry
You sank deeper and deeper into her
Puncturing deeper into my hurt
Could you feel my low
        from your high?
From her scream
        could you hear my cry?
Could you feel me breaking
        as you reached your goal?
Or did you ignore the thought of me
        racing to the surface of your mind?

And as you fucked her
I have to ask
In what colour did you write "fuck you"
To the girl you left behind?

I held our bomb all by myself most days
It was heavy and inevitably
counting down the seconds to our demise
Nonetheless I held us tight to my chest
cherishing what we built all by myself
ignoring any signs that lit up a goodbye
We were supposed to work together
to defuse our destruction
But instead you sped up the process
with lies and deception
The explosion came as a complete surprise
I believed you up until the very last second
Now I know better for next time
That real love uses no weapon

ACHE

noun

a continuous or prolonged dull pain in a part of
one's body.

such as the heart.

My heart aches for me almost as much as she aches for you.

Yesterday was easier
When you were still with her
Today has gotten harder
So I wish that you still were

See I like it when you're wrapped up in a
steady relationship
For otherwise I think up all the ways we could fit

My imagination has been known to get the best of me
And my subconscious mind is good at taking over all
of me

I picture you
Way late at night
And hold you still
Come morning light
But when I wake
I realize
I see your face
Not next to mine

Could it be
That this whole time
It was just me
With you in my mind

You clutter all my thoughts
And you take up all my time
So I'd just like to know
If you'd consider being mine

It's 3:00 a.m. And I can't sleep, again. So I grab my journal and this green pen. I would like to blame my new piercing, annoying my left ear, and the fact that I can't sleep on it. Or the fresh ink on my right ribcage, and the fact that I can't sleep on it. But the truth is, I just can't sleep. And it's been this way since before the tattoo, and before the piercing.

You were a prisoner. Someone I made into a bad guy and locked up in a cell in the back of my mind. But then you start coming around in reality and reminding me that you aren't bad at all. So I peek.

I peek at you in your cell and at all the memories that go along with you. And they start flooding. They creep up on me when I wake up, and fifty times throughout my day. And finally, at 3:00 a.m., when I once slept peacefully with you as prisoner, deep in the back of my mind in your cell. But now, I wake up each night to you wandering the halls of my thoughts, holding me prisoner of my own mind.

At the end of all these thoughts, as my eyes begin to cross, I think maybe you should be here. I could tell you all of this, and you could get annoyed by me disrupting your sleep at 3:00 a.m. and hold me until I fell asleep once again. Why does there always have to be a prisoner?

I'll throw away a boy as if he doesn't have the guts to love,
But I'm the one who's gutless, 'cause I throw away the
ones I trust.

you remember everything I say,

and I wish you wouldn't.

because I say way too much,

way too often.

I get carried away

in spilling my truths.

I continually confess,

while you continually listen.

and I wish you wouldn't.

this colour reminds me of you
I used to write about you in it
a fairly simple shade of blue
when our sky, it had no limits

I bought a book the other day
knowing damn well I'd find you in it
my fingers linger on each page
to turn would mean I'd have to finish

my path in life gets crossed
with things that remind me of you
but blaming "things" for all my thoughts
would be a lie, and I can't face the truth

The truth is I think about you all the same
when we met and fell into it
feelings fade but never change
you're still the one I'd like to be with

You've gotten my hopes up,
once again.
You seem to do this every time
you let me in.
You and I, we get closer,
then you make it seem like
it's the end.
And the finger points toward,
"we're too delicate."
Quite possibly,
I've made this whole thing up
in my head.
Where now you don't want me,
where I am simply
misled.
But you've gotten my hopes up.
So I'm hoping I'm
correct.
That you and I belong,
even when
we're too delicate.

I told him I would wait. Well, I told him that I'm not looking elsewhere, and I don't care to. I've spent the last year, or four, discovering myself and not really looking elsewhere. And all that time has led me right back where I started: to him. And all this time, I thought I had come so far, and I have. So, how is it, he shows up and takes me right back to the beginning? And now I have nothing better to do but to wait. But what if he takes his time now, discovers himself and discovers I'm not what he wants or needs. What if everything I've been through led me back to him, and he's about to go through everything that will lead him away from me.

sometimes I can't tell
whether my stomach's knots
are its way of adjusting
to all the words I lost
when I told them to you
or if all the words I didn't say
are in tangles
wishing I would give them to you

How do you grasp what love is when the person you love is so far out of your grasp?

It's never the love
or the attachment
I shy away from.
It's all the things
I'm expected
to give to you,
once we've proclaimed
such affections.

I'm nearing the
bottom of this
bottle of wine
as I'm realizing
all the
feelings
I
h
a
v
e
b
e
e
n
bottling inside

Nowadays,
I say, we fell in love,
with a smile on my face.
As if to say, we still are.

Let's be honest, we would've been perfect. We were perfect. You grounded me, and I elevated you. We were balanced. So what happened? Did I want to watch you fly? As if you were the balloon, when I thought you were the bird. Did I let go of your string before you could figure out how to grow wings? I can see it now. Me, "setting you free." And you, drifting into an endless blue, watching me grow smaller and smaller. And there was nothing you could do about it. I'm the one who should have held on. I'm the one who let go. You must hate me. Don't you? I know I would hate me. But once you lost all the oxygen you had, and you floated back down to the ground, you were the one to let me resuscitate you. But I was under the impression I was giving CPR to a bird, when really, I was trying to re-inflate a popped balloon. How silly I must have looked to you.

brandi marie

but if a heart breaks
in the same way
more than twice
was it ever truly healed
in the first place?

I'm questioning it all,
from where I rise, to how I fall.
Because although I've found myself here,
I still long to be wherever you are.

I suppose when I'm on my own,
this is where my pieces can hold.
But I'm better held by you.
Even if you think you're unglued.

See, I don't only want you when you're whole.
I'm not only in this to be set to cruise control.
I want to love you in between understanding yourself.
I want to be by your side through it all.

I'm at ease with myself,
and torn apart over you.
I'm out here finding myself,
wondering if I'll ever get over you.

If I ever even want to.

How could I ever fall out of love with you?

His ghost washes over me like a season.
I miss him when he's gone.
And when his ghost is present,
He demands to be felt.
Like the hot sunshine.
Or the crisp snowfall.
Like a warm rain.
He makes me feel it all.

I'm trying not to take it personally,
when no one I want, wants to be with me.
And I'm trying to blame myself
for being so alone.
For it is my fault to deny the loves
who turn and reach to me.
But the ones I want always turn and run,
claiming they need to set me free.
Maybe they were never meant
to stay in my life.
Maybe I was meant
to walk through theirs.
Maybe I have something bigger
to learn
than allowing boys
to spill all my tears.
I want something real,
but I know I can't force it.
I want to feel something
to make it all worth it.
But I guess it is my fault
for being the one who skipped town.
And only I'm to blame
for being so tough to tie down.
But the truth is, if I stayed,
he would've picked her anyways.

brandi marie

there

is

a

part

of

me

that

hates

her

for

getting

him

for

the

same

part

of

me

is

incapable

of

forgetting

him

I was wondering if you knew
about this feeling you give me
where my legs feel unsteady
like they know not to plant themselves
in case you decide to take it all back
and change your mind
it's happened before
so I'm ready for it
I still don't want this outcome
but my legs are ready to run

the times are changing
and the time has changed
now it's dark before five
and it always rains
I knew this would happen
it's just always too soon
like the change in your heart
leaving me without you

People like you tend to take what they want.
I tend to shy away from people like you.
Because people like you scare me.

I am the type of person to give
Only when others earn, when they are deserving.
Otherwise, I fear they may damage what is my beauty.

I refuse to allow you entry
Upon a sacred place such as my soft heart.
The door is locked.

But if you choose to prove your worth,
You may find I will lend you the key
To my dangerously soft heart.

brandi marie

You're going to have to learn how to share my heart
with them.
And I don't mean in a physical,
Or even in a this-dimensional kind of way.
I mean that they have pieces of my heart
when I don't have them.
So I can't give you all of something
That I barely have half of.

tight throat
knotted stomach
all the signs
that I feel too much
gravity fails
to hold me down
light conversation
yet I start to drown
"no hard feelings"
what does that even mean
I don't know what I'm feeling
but I can't seem to breathe
"how are you?"
"I'm good" "that's great"
"what about you?"
"same here" but it's fake
this entire conversation
feels it could be the last one
and I'm shaking I'm anxious
I don't want us to be done
I know I need some closure
I also know I want you closer
but it's finally sinking in
that this whole thing is really over

189

brandi marie

I hate
feeling like I can't say
what I want to say
without it getting back to you
in some negative way.

I know I'll say yes
When I want to say no
I just want you to know
That I'm wearing the dress
With the hole in the back
That I wore to impress you
The first day that we met
You know the one
It's all black
There's just one little difference
My hair's in a mess
'Cause I just can't seem to
Get myself out of bed
I know you'll be there
At this stupid event
But you won't be with me
Won't be holding your hand
On the small of my back
Through the hole in my dress
'Cause instead you'll just be
This big hole in my chest
Just know if you called me
Right now and asked me
To drop all my plans
And go with you instead
I'd want to say no
But you know
I'll say yes

brandi marie

And my chest still hurts

When I think about you with her

Because I think about you with me

And how we were so happy

It isn't fair

And I should not care

But I do

I do because it's you

You'd think it would be easier for me to forget you
seeing as you aren't the same you whom I can't forget

And you'd think it'd be harder for you to forget me
seeing as I haven't changed since the first day we met

brandi marie

I want to say I'm sorry
That I don't truly like you
I want to say I'm sorry
But I don't think that's the truth

I want to say I'm sorry
And I truly want to mean that
But I don't want to say a damn thing
If I don't really feel it

—no apologies are better than fake ones

I held onto you so tight
   that you s

         l

           i

              p

                p

                  e

                    d

through my grip
like sand in the summer
once my lover
now another's

dusk to dawn
hearts to sand
curtains drawn
out of my hands

brandi marie

I would tell you
but
I don't want to get in between
anything you have going on with
her
not that I don't think we'd be
great
just that too often I tend to
change my mind
and if that ended up being the
case
I wouldn't want her getting
hurt for
no reason other than how
selfish
I can be
you are good and so am I but
so is she
I would tell you how I feel about
you
or at least how I think I feel but
this
is how I feel
and I feel as though you already

know

I'm admitting things I never thought were true.
I'm admitting things that I would never say to you.
I'll tell the world until word gets back to you.
But if you didn't hear it from me,
would you still believe it to be true?

How: words from my mouth
become word of mouth.

Our first breakup was like watching the sun set on summer solstice. A long, beautiful goodbye, that (I don't know about you, but) I held onto, hoping it would last, knowing it would come back. Every time after that (as days do following summer solstice) grew shorter. Your patience for me grew thinner. No longer could you be bothered to hold the weight of the sun up as I pushed it down on us. Eventually, you were the one to climb above the sun and force it along with gravity as I watched, knowing this is how I made you feel. Except you never just stood watch. You always fought to please me, or rather to appease yourself. A world without continuous light was the one you grew up in, and the one you never intended to create. And I'm sorry for sealing our fate as one you so strongly hated. My only excuse is my selfish side being unwilling to get enough of the beautiful love we created. But you and I both were never much for sunsets anyways.

I always imagined my thoughts revolving around you would fade along with the scent of your cologne I used to spray onto my sweaters. But they've long smelt only of me and my washing machine, while my thoughts still revolve only around you.

brandi marie

I poured all my heart out.
I did it,
again.

You told me
you wanted to be more
than just friends.

But when I asked you
for patience,
you jumped the gun.

You could've waited;
I wanted this
to be love.

I know you didn't mean it
in the same way that I took it,
but I swear that everything you do
indirectly affects me.

damaged, damnit.

Does it really take
me being happy,
and settling down with
someone, for you to
realize that you wish
you would've waited
for me to reach this
point with you?

And maybe if I couldn't (already) predict your reaction to what I don't want to say, I'd say it.

I love the colours in the morning. The soft pink skyline cut through by the distant blue mountains. The bold yellow sunrise seeping over all who dare to disrupt her path. I love the sparkle off the water, and the shimmer of the dew. I love the glisten off the cars and how it makes me think of you. The way you used to kiss me, before I'd opened up my eyes. Making me feel things before I even felt alive. You used to make me breakfast as I wrote about your smile. But the colours keep on changing, closing in on all these miles.

How
many
times
must
I
feel

                                        unwanted

before
someone
makes
me
feel
wanted

                                —I'm over here

And now I work at the place we used to drink red wine. And I can't take it when a stranger orders what you used to have next to me. But I also can't take it to forget and let all our memories slip like red wine on your soft lips.

sometimes
    I forget
        all the things
            I said to you
                in my head

                sometimes
        I wish
      you were there
   to hear it
all of it

my boyfriend keeps pictures of
his ex in a drawer, which makes
me wonder if I'm still in yours.

Sometimes, I close my eyes and I'm back
on that floaty in the middle of
Sunrise Lake lying next to you
looking up at the stars and
wishing that we were closer
even though we are or were
yet feeling closer to the stars
even though they were so far
away.

I wish I had you
Back when I had him
Then I could have him
Now that I have you

—An unfair trade

Dreams
are truly awful things
when they disguise themselves
as good
as sweet

I held you in my arms last night
I had you back inside my heart

but Dreams
are truly awful things
when they hide your fears
in fantasies

you were the one I wanted to love
but you left me for her because

I'm
Never
Enough

Why do you always
reach out to me when
I least expect it, and
expect me not to be
affected?

as soon as the film ends,

I know I should've turned it off sooner.

Because it ends the way I wish the scene between you and me had ended.

Except you and I ended much, much sooner.

I know that I'm going to be fine
But that doesn't mean it doesn't still hurt sometimes

brandi marie

HEAL

verb

to become whole or sound; mend; get well (often fol-
lowed by up or over).

Mom says, "That's healing up nicely,"
as she examines the scrape on your knee.
And you look up at her, confusedly.
Why did she use the words "healing up,"
when it so obviously has scabbed over?
"Won't there be a scar?" you wonder.
You can't help but wonder.
"Not if you don't pick at it." Her words are stern.
So you try as hard as you can to leave it alone.
Or do you?
No, that isn't right.
You never know how to leave well enough alone,
and you have a body full of scars to prove it.

The thing about scars
is they were once painful
or bleeding
or at the very least uncomfortable

But once they have healed
we tend to forget where they came from

cobwebs.

if you'd like to call a
truce,
then I'd like to call an
end.
I'm over feeling
used,
you seem to never
bend.
I am not your
fool,
and you are not my
friend.
I wish you only
knew,
that bitter is my
extent.
perhaps I played my hand
too soon,
to stop the cycle, which we're
in.
but it comes down to me and
you,
and how we'll never learn to
mend.
these broken pieces are all
strewn,
the carpet is stained in black and
red.
I wish to clear you from my
room,
and wipe the cobwebs from my
chest.

I'd like to take a piece of you,
And place it back into my heart.
Not a part that belongs to you,
But a piece that used to be me.

I was always too bold for you.
I outshined you while you were trying to be a bright star.
And I did it without trying.

You liked me.
But you liked yourself just a little bit more.

You wanted me,
And I was all for it.
But you never wanted me the way I wanted you.

And I'll admit that I enjoy being the brightest one in
a duo.
But I never imagined someone would deny me,
For wanting the same thing.

I couldn't hold onto that
Any more than you wouldn't hold onto me.
And it's a shame.

Through my eyes,
You were already a bright star.
And that's exactly how you saw me too.
But I was always too bold for you.

My heart is in need of a recipe
Maybe one cup of sugar
Two of flour
What is now solely mine
Used to be ours
A whole block of butter
One teaspoon baking powder
One pinch of cinnamon
But don't overpower
I was so used to you and me
I'd forgotten myself
So knead me until
I don't need anyone else
Heat up the oven
But don't burn me now
I must rise
I must bake
All fluffy and brown
With every shattered piece of my heart
And a tablespoon of honey
I will come out the other side
And I will learn how to love me

You've gotten too used to having someone.
You've forgotten how to be your very own one.

Maybe they aren't the ones to blame for my love-
less attitude.
Perhaps I'm too much of a hopeless romantic,
Who holds onto the past longer and tighter than I ought.
Maybe if I was more inviting, love would do the same.
Perhaps if I took down my walls,
Someone would have the chance to prove me wrong.

But all these "maybes"
And "perhapses"
Are simply me being too proud to admit
That I've been living wrong.
Or rather,
I've been loving wrong.
Not that there is necessarily a wrong way to love,
But there is wrong in the way I block out love.

So, maybe,
Perhaps,
Certainly,
I should try to let go of my idea of a happy ending,
And allow myself an unfamiliar new beginning.

The healing process is so ugly.

Let's be honest here.

Even the paper cuts are cringeworthy

And I find myself cutting limes far too often.

But the bullet wounds,

The screams,

The blood.

It's not pretty.

The miscarriages,

The despair,

The presence of hopelessness.

It's not romantic.

So let's be honest here.

The healing process is ugly.

And each wound demands a different way to be felt,

To be treated,

And to be healed.

But even between the gritting of his teeth,

The dried-out tears on her face,

The open mouth with no scream left to come out,

And the clenched fists ready to do more harm to them-
selves than to anyone else.

It's all ugly.

But those scars can turn out to be so beautiful if you
let them.

I washed the last of you off my body just now in cold, cold water. I don't know what else to tell you, other than how damn good it felt. And I guess how you're never going to feel this body again. Because I'm no longer capable of feeling your body, without imagining hers there too. And whether you prefer the touch of this other girl over my own touch. And how every time I've touched you from here on, I've given up another ounce of self-respect. And how I'm unwilling to give any more of myself to you. I think you've taken enough. I just wanted you to know that my body no longer possesses your dirty fingerprints. And this is me, clearing you of my thoughts too.

—fingerprints sliding down the drain

there is too much here between us
there is too much past
and too much love
we hold on too much
but I don't want to be done

I know you crave a fresh start
a new face full of young love
and I know I miss you too much
and I was never enough

but there is not enough here between us
there is not enough fight
and not enough love
we've let go enough
it's about time we wake up

I want to hold on
because there is something between us
yet you're letting go
claiming we're no longer in love

there is too much here between us
there is too much past
and too much love
we've held on enough
it's about time we let up

And when he breaks your heart
for the millionth time,

Remember,
you've already been through this.

tell me something personal
something that hurts for me to know
the names of all your hidden ghosts
it's time to learn how to let them go

I'm waiting to be found
And yet I know that no one is looking
I'm waiting to be crowned
And yet I'm not even in the running
I'm waiting for my prince
And yet I'm nowhere near royalty
I'm waiting for true love's first kiss
And yet no one is dreaming of me
I'm waiting for things
That aren't bound to happen
Unless I stop waiting
Stop believing in magic

I'm sorry for wasting your time,
But I'm no longer interested in wasting mine.

Be careful
With how many times
You allow your heart to break
Although your heart is a muscle
It heals like a bone
Growing stronger
After every time
It has to put itself back together
And there is no heart
More resistant
To falling in love
Than one that has been broken

Like the fear of
Re-breaking a bone
Hearts stand against
The vulnerability to fall again
So be careful
But always consider
You will grow stronger
Every time you fall
And love
And break

May your last lover
Receive the strongest heart
You are capable of creating

I liked it when you took my hand,
and told me we would never land.
But you're a boy, not a man,
and I'm not Wendy, Peter Pan.

You cannot stop what has been done.
But you can stop the satisfaction that your reaction will
give to whomever did it.

Perhaps I have learned how to wait it out
Like a spontaneous summer storm swooping through
the valley
There I am
Taking refuge beneath a tree

I don't think you understand just how far I have come
I used to chase after your storms
I believed I could outrun them
I could find solace where the sun still shone
But chasing after storms only keeps you at their mercy
That much longer

And the thing about storms
Especially when it comes to yours if I'm to blame
Continue to only grow angrier
And angrier
I have accepted that there is no escaping
Your annual torrential downpour
And I have decided to embrace it

I have finally stopped trying to exist beneath your
dark clouds
Now I dance through your storms
For the hell of it
For the memories
For I know it won't last

you got so damn close to me

I wanted to cry

but the memory seemed so distant

I guess it healed over time

brandi marie

Don't feel guilty.

Do whatever it is you need to do,

In order to heal.

If you need to act out, act out.

If you need to kiss someone else, kiss someone else.

If you need to hide somewhere no one can find you, start looking for a good hiding spot.

And, my dear, if you need to cry, don't let anyone tell you that you're weak.

One of the hardest parts about
opening up your heart again
is remembering that you're only opening it up
for one new person.
And all the people you wish
you could still let in,
are the reason you had to learn how to
re-open your heart
in the first place.

Please, don't ever think that I left you because I didn't love you,
or that I just didn't love you enough.
And don't believe for a second that you didn't love me enough,
or that you could've ever loved me more.
Because all it comes down to
is how I didn't love me enough.
And compared to how much you loved me,
I needed to learn to love myself just as much.

I never realized the extent of your love for me,
until I learned to love myself just as much.

Be gentle
Because when you treat something poorly after it has
been damaged
It only means
You never cared for it in the first place

So be gentle
The way you would after accidentally dropping something
That is worth the world to you
The way you ought to treat a heart

Remember, you are who you are
Because of who left you behind
But you're the one who got yourself this far
No one else gets to decide

Take a bath
And cry your eyes out
Lie awake
All night overthinking
Call your best friend
And tell her every detail
Dress up
And go out drinking
Stay in bed
With takeout and a hangover
Buy new shoes
Or a car to treat yourself
Change your hair
Until he doesn't recognize you
And if nothing else works
Chocolate helps

brandi marie

Healing does take time
And just for the record
You will never be the same
Being healed doesn't mean being cured
It doesn't mean nothing happened
It means something indeed did happen
And you're still around to tell the story

Yet you live your life in a way that prevents the same
wound from ever occurring twice
And that kind of precaution is the true scar on your heart

⚠CAUTION

brandi marie

When your heart gets broke
You're left feeling naked
Bare
Exposed

You're so vulnerable
That you're angry
Hurt
And low

But after you regain
Your petrified pride
And discard
Your shame

You get to
Dress your naked body
In any way you desire
You get to choose

Healing can be beautiful

A nurse log is a fallen, decaying tree, who provides an ecological home for new vegetation. It offers nutrients, shade, water, protection, a safe place for new life to be reborn. It's so fascinating how something once so grand can fall and sprout new life and new meaning. I have had a few great loves, and each time one falls, it leaves a space behind for the next to grow.

brandi marie

Maybe it hurts so badly
That you cut off all ties
That even remotely
Remind you of him

Then maybe you distract
Yourself with hobbies
Until you're so sidetracked
You aren't thinking of him

Then maybe you get so wrapped up
In things you love
That you forget
That you love him

Then maybe you see him
And you say hi
Because it no longer hurts you
When he walks by

Healing doesn't always mean you don't love that
person anymore
It simply means you've accepted it's possible to love
another more

There is no countdown
Or a set amount of time
There is no celebration
Or toast to being fine

There is no congratulations
You've made it out alive
There is no relief
After you've had to say goodbye

Unlike graduation
Or passing that exam
Unlike a promotion
Or sharing engagement plans

Healing goes unnoticed
Even on a CT scan
You have to reward yourself
For being confident without a man

When did your mom stop putting the Band-Aids on
for you?
And why wasn't that a big deal?
And why do you need her now more than ever?
As if, without Mom's kiss, this wound won't heal.
It's because you *know* that paper cut will mend;
You've been through it before.
But this is something you hope *she's* been through;
To prove to you, it's going to be okay.
Isn't that what moms are for?

Remember when your dad laughed at you
When you fell off your bike?
And how he felt so bad afterwards,
Once he realized you'd cried.
Would you call it funny now, or ironic,
That you're crying out all your feelings,
And all you want is for him to laugh at you?
To remind you that it's not a big deal;
To prove to you, it's going to be okay.
Isn't that what dads are for?

brandi marie

It would be easier, wouldn't it,
If there were a perfectly defined diagnosis?
Here it is, here is what is wrong with you.
Take these orange pills and ditch your blues.

It would be easier, wouldn't it?
You could stop thinking of yourself as broken.
Keep the cast on for two weeks,
Then we'll take it off, and let it breathe.

It would be easier, wouldn't it,
If someone could stop you from choking?
The Heimlich manoeuvre, round one, two, three.
And it all comes out, your throat is free.

It would be easier, wouldn't it,
To have anything, anything but heartache?
To be healed by medicine or Band-Aids, instead of time.
To be ill in bed and still call him mine.

If all it takes is time,

Why does it take so much out of me?

My mom would always plant the rotten bananas under
her roses.
To help them grow.
And they would bloom in spring, but come
winter, decompose.
The dead thorns wouldn't be half as beautiful until coated
in snow.
That's how I felt after you and I had froze.
And I guess something had to die in order for me to
blossom full.
And I guess some things only a mother knows.
Like why rotten bananas help roses to grow.

When you get the flu,

The doctor recommends bed rest and fluids.

And, may I suggest,

You treat your heart like it has the flu?

Don't look for someone to heal you.

Give your heart time to rest and renew.

There is this song
That always makes me cry
Of course it's not the song
It's obviously the guy
But every time it comes on
I can't turn it off
I have to listen and to wonder
Why wasn't I enough
So I listen to this song
I listen all the way through
Wiping tears off my face
Tears that came from you
If I could mail it in letter
And send this song your way
I wonder if you'd cry too
Or would you simply just downplay
Downplay how much it means
How each word touches your heart
Downplay the way you left
Left me here to hurt
Every time this song comes on
I cry one tear less
I wipe away the thought of you
And get used to how you left

Heal me from this broken heart
And take away the pain.
Is all this hurt from you, my love,
Or is it all in vain?

brandi marie

Closure You Probably Don't Need

I left you because you knew who I was
And I had no idea
I couldn't tell if it was because
You knew me that well
Or you knew how to paint my picture

I left you because I needed to find out
How to be independent
After two years beneath you
I didn't know how
I craved to bear the weight of my world
On my shoulders
And my shoulders alone

And here's what I learned

I left you to climb mountains
To write songs and poems
I left you to be reckless
To break hearts like mine was broken
I left you to trade dancing for dirt biking
To trade skating for snowboarding
To trade vulnerability for valiance
To trade the white-picket fence
For white-water rafting

I learned that I am more than naiveté
I am more than a dream
I am life and adventure
I rip dreams at their seams
I learned all my limits

When to stay or head home
I learned that you loved me
More than I'll ever know

I wasn't the only one who left
I know you left me too
But I had to dive into myself
Find out who I could be without you

So I left you because you knew who I was
And I had no idea
But you left me because I was finding out
And the me you knew so well
Left you with amnesia

THRIVE

verb

to grow or develop vigorously; flourish.

"Am I happy?" she asks herself, after years of associating happiness with love. And to finally have found love, she ought to have discovered happiness as well,

Right?

Or is it possible that those years of desperately wanting to be loved, experiencing disappointment, and inevitably giving up, led her to herself? Turning all that outward energy in and finding peace there?

She found a lover after she learned how to love herself.

But she found happiness first.

I was happy with him
I was happy with the him before him
And guess what
I'll be happy again
Without him

My plan is to publish this
Regardless
Of what you think
I hope you can see past the pain
And appreciate the hand you played
In creating what I like to call art
I hope you see the significance in your part
And if you don't
My plan is to publish this
Regardless
Of what you think

I had opened my doors up so wide for your love, how could you blame me when he entered, carrying everything I wanted, everything that you refused to give to me? How could you blame me when my doors closed and you never moved from your place on my porch?

How could you blame me?

The reason my doors were even opened in the first place was for you. The reason they closed was for all the things you didn't do.

How could you?

You let me tear open a heart I had so strategically sewn back together. You led me to believe you would be there when I did, holding us both together. But you weren't there.

And he was.

And he wasn't just convenient. And you weren't just not there. He was everything I ever wanted from you. He was everything I had been looking for. I just didn't realize I was looking in the wrong places, until I looked away from you.

brandi marie

After all our bad blood had settled,
I think we were brought together one last time
To realize that we've healed.
We've healed from being torn apart,
From all the stabs we had taken to our hearts.
We've healed from all the sleepless nights,
Laid down our defences brought up to fight.
I've healed from every single ache that formed,
That broke over the mention of your name.
You've healed from rage and doused the fire,
To cease igniting your late-night desires.
We built ourselves up, tall and strong.
But we knew our weak points all along.
I kicked the walls; you tore them down.
Now, here we are, four feet on the ground.
We've come so far; we've touched the stars,
But all that's left are fading scars.
We had love once; you loved me twice,
And I'll love you forever against all advice.
But after all our bad blood had settled,
I think we were brought together one last time
To realize that we've healed.
We may finally forgive each other,
And fully appreciate what we had together.

The best revenge is when they realize you are happier without them.

I Don't Plan To Hold My Breath
I Don't Want To Keep Confessing
But You're The One Who Knows Me Best
And I Know That You'll Keep Me Guessing

How Am I To Walk Away
From Eyes That Keep On Begging Me
If They Could Speak I'd Hear Their Plea
Instead I Hear No Just Leave

So I Move On But You're Still Here
At Parties I Still Catch Your Stare
Eyes Can't Lie The Way Mouths Dare
Deep Underneath I See You Care

Quiet Now As I Paint Out The Rest
One Day You'll Realize I Know You Best
But As You Close In To Confess
I Won't Be There
Won't Be Holding My Breath

Does he make you happy?

I left the girl who kept choosing
to be with someone
who didn't make her happy
behind
the day I stopped choosing
to be with you.

I make decisions and then I live with them
I change my mind and then I go back again
I change course and then I adapt and grow
I realize I'm wrong and then I let go

Nothing is permanent not even this pen
But even if it were, I would write this again
You can walk away whenever you want
Or stay where you are for as long as you want

People get hurt and people move on
But people love love, so people hold on
Just listen to your heart, that's all I try to do
And if someone can't love you, then you have to love you

Sometimes I write to an audience,

And sometimes I write solely to you.

As if, no matter who reads my words,

You will hear them as if I spoke them to you.

Can you tell

When my words are meant for your heart?

Can you tell

When I'm screaming that we got torn apart!

Can you tell

That this is my means of healing, of moving on?

Can you tell

That because of these words, I'm thriving and calm?

Because when I write to an audience,

I have something to share.

But when I write to you,

It's like a lift in the air.

I write out the closure that you never gave.

And I write out my future that I get to pave.

I write out my fears, my worries, and greys.

But not only do I write them down,

I write them away.

I write to you,

To write you away.

Everything I love to do
Wasn't in my life
Until I walked away from you

I won't ever apologize for writing my truths.
I won't ever regret walking away from you.
I bet the truth hurts almost as much as your lies do.
I won't ever apologize if my truths hurt you.

I loved you once.
Maybe even more than once.
And I still experience nostalgia over you,
More than once a year.
Un-admittedly, I'm admitting things,
If you read between these lines.
I know you won't,
Which is why I will.
But when you get through this poem,
And when I get through my tears,
We will both realize
Why I put my thoughts to words
And left them here.
It's not for you.
They never were.

You broke my heart once.
Maybe even more than once.
But all that heartache
Has graduated into nostalgia over the years.
And it's not over you.
Sometimes, I reflect on the girl you once knew.
More than once.
And sometimes, I wish you knew me now.
Like how I'll always know you.

I don't want to need
someone who needs me
to feel they're happy
that's not love to me

I don't want to be
someone that you need
but if you want me
that'd be cool with me

Sometimes, we hide from the world
When we're sad, scared, or stressed,
Dealing with pain, grief,
Or whilst getting undressed.

But when you run from the world
And hide from the crowds,
You're only fooling yourself
When you "don't want to be found."

I would know.
I've tried hiding all my wounds.
But they never cease to bleed
Until they're kissed by you.

Stop hiding in places;
Start running to faces.

You forgot to pause

You pressed rewind and play so many times
On someone who fast-forwarded beyond you

I get it if you didn't want to keep playing
On the same roll of tape as a story that ended

But you could've pressed pause

Just for a moment
Until you figured out how to change the tape

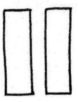

my exes aren't jealous,
but their girlfriends always are.

maybe art is our heart's way of apologizing for all the discomfort and confusion she caused our minds. maybe art is our heart's interpretation to uniquely justify her destructive performances. maybe art is our heart's explanation, simplifying the reasons we ought to listen to her, time and time again. maybe art is the answer to every question we pose, without exposing herself; without taking off her clothes. maybe art can only be felt by a heart held in another's, by a heart broken by another's. maybe art is our heart's way of communicating; of speaking words she was never taught how to say. and when we never introduce any concept, apart from the truth, our hearts create art out of what she knows best: you and love.

Can we worry less
And take life at face value;
Can we not stress
Over anything that is not true;
Can we leave the mess
That we've made in the past;
Can we not confess
And invite such overcast?
Let's worry less
And spend time in the sun.
There's no need to stress;
Life only gave us one.

I only write from within my heart.
So, if I don't write about you,
It shows exactly where you aren't.

you may be a poem,
        but I am your poet.

you may be a work of art,
        but I am your artist.

maybe you live on
        within my song,

but you are not my chorus.

maybe I draw inspiration
        from your lies,

but I am the one who is honest.

I am not the type of girl

who can go all in

for something that will never be

more than half-hearted

What is life after love?
After heartache?

How do you move on?
Is there an end to all the healing?

Maybe not wholly.
Maybe not entirely.

But there are moments.

Moments when you are as far from love as you possibly
can be,
And you are happier than you ever were in it.

Even if it's just one song.
One drive.
One night.
Or one smile.

That one moment
Is you,
In all your glory.
Needing no one
But yourself.

When you learn that loving yourself is the best thing you can do for yourself,

that is when you truly learn what love is.

And when you do have someone
You don't need to rely on them
To make you happy

That's your job

Their job is to accompany you when you're not happy
Their job is to laugh with you when you are
Their job is to see the good in you
And remind you what that looks like when you forget
But your job is to show them the good in you
That you fought for
For who knows how many years until it shone out of you
Like sunshine

I put all my eggs in one basket
So to speak
Yours
Of course
And you were like stone
You wouldn't budge an inch
Not for me
It wasn't the first time either
This has happened to us before
But unlike the last few times
When I waited relentlessly
Hopelessly
I left
I packed a few things
And I left everything else
And everyone
Including you
Behind me
I moved away
Literally
I moved on
Forcefully
I wasn't going to sit around waiting for you
Waiting to become someone
When I could gain everything I needed from you
From me
Just by allowing myself some space
And following my inner compass to a new place
Where I could be anyone I wanted
A fresh start
But instead
I was just me
And it finally felt right

We need to work on loving ourselves more
More than the effort we put into drawing love into
our lives

We need to realize we don't need a relationship to
be successful
We don't need love to be fulfilled

But if I didn't learn to love
Or allow myself to be loved

You wouldn't be reading this book

you need to love you
before you ask me to

brandi marie

some people prefer
being admired from afar
to recognize beauty
enclosed in a jar

some people enjoy
being held in the dark
to be felt and not seen
without touching one's heart

although I like to be seen
and enjoy being touched
there is only one way
this heart feels like enough

I like to be heard
so please try to listen
my trophies are words
especially those I have written

I like my own belongings better when they appear to belong to someone. After being used. Worn-out, ripped jeans. Empty bottles of beer. Those bulging, over-full journals. Pleated, wrinkly, cozy crew necks. Tarnished wood on the coffee table. Creased or bent or folded books and their pages. Matted and obviously cuddled teddy bears.

Loved and broken hearts.

My belongings go through life as I do. I go through loving them, feeling like I've ruined them, and then learn to re-love them despite their flaws; despite what I've put them through.

A scratched-out word on my otherwise perfect page of poetry. A coffee stain on the edges of my favourite book. The chip in my small front tooth to remind me of a fun night out with friends and too many drinks.

Flaws add character.

Imperfections add personality.

Scars add experience.

When you learn to love the things you've ruined, you learn they aren't ruined at all, but made. They're made into beauty, into art. My heart is quite like this.

It was once young, carefree, innocent, hopeful, and imaginative. It's since grown cold, dark, broken, and re-broken. And now, it beats. After all I have put it through. It heals, loves, and re-loves. My heart has experience, personality, and character. My heart is its very own work of art.

What finish line?

You can't cross something that ceases to exist.

As human beings, we are always evolving.

Always growing.

And if you think you're there,

You're wrong.

There is no finish line.

I learned I had to dig deep
I had to get mud underneath my fingernails
I had to crawl on my hands and knees
Through the tunnel I created

I learned I had to mine
I had to chisel away at the cracks in the walls
I had to strike away at myself until I hit something hard
Until I pushed back

I learned I had to take a hit
I had to be tougher than I thought I was capable of being
I had to surpass golds and silvers
Until all that was left were diamonds

I learned I had to work hard
I had to become the best version of myself
I had to dig non-stop
Until I was satisfied

brandi marie

I still remember how badly it hurt when I walked away from you.

I remember thinking to myself: this horrible heartache will fade. There is no way it will always hurt this badly.

But I was wrong.

Although it hurts less frequently as time trudges along, every now and then I feel like I did that first day. Just the same.

I've slept more nights without you then I ever did next to you. Yet I still lose sleep over you.

I wish it were different. I wish time could actually heal.

Now that I know it can't, I wish I could turn it back to that day I first hurt, to tell myself: this horrible heartache will never fade. There is no way you will ever get over this, over him.

And I would fix it. I would stay.

And I would miss out on every other experience, and every other lesson since.

I would be with you.

But would I still be me?

sometimes the best
part of loving some
one else is learning
from them how to
l o v e   y o u r s e l f

When I left you, the very first time, I left for me. I had so much to discover and become. And on that day, I told you that I wished for thoughts of me to make you think of the sun. I wanted to be bright and beautiful to you. The way you saw me, mattered. Because the way you saw me was in a light I could not see myself. You saw me for who I was before I even knew who I was. And I never understood that. Until I met her. The girl you fell in love with. She is bold and unique, and you are the only one who can make her weak. She is confident and spontaneous; she is never set on one thing unless that one thing is us. She's an artist, but she gets stumped. Yet her art seems to bloom when you're her inspiration. She has been a closed door to all who have knocked, and your hand holds the key to her heart that's been locked. I've discovered myself; I have grown and become. On my own, I am bold, and I shine like the sun. It took time to learn this, but now my learning is done. Now I love who I am, and I know who I love.

It is anything but easy
To be anything but
There isn't much between
Being hurt or in love
From one to the next
With no time to breathe
How can we excel
When we don't feel complete
We feel whole when there's two of us
And half once that ends
So this is where I explore the part
Where I mend
Where I take time to ache
And I take time to heal
And after all that work
I show you how I feel
I can recognize my hurt
And acknowledge my fears
Give independence my grace
And calm my own tears
I find myself singing
With no reason at all
And I catch myself smiling
At my readiness to fall
I've never been happier alone
I've never felt more alive
Than when I gave myself time
To ache
Heal
Then thrive

A Note from the Author

Thank you for going through the cycle of love and heart-break with me. Wherever you are, personally, within the stages, I hope you embrace it. I hope that even in the heat of the fight and the ache of the loneliness, you know you will be okay again. Love is a cycle worth going through. I also appreciate being able to go through it with you.

Brandi Marie

Instagram: @brandimariepoetry
Email: brandimariepoetry@gmail.com

Printed in Canada